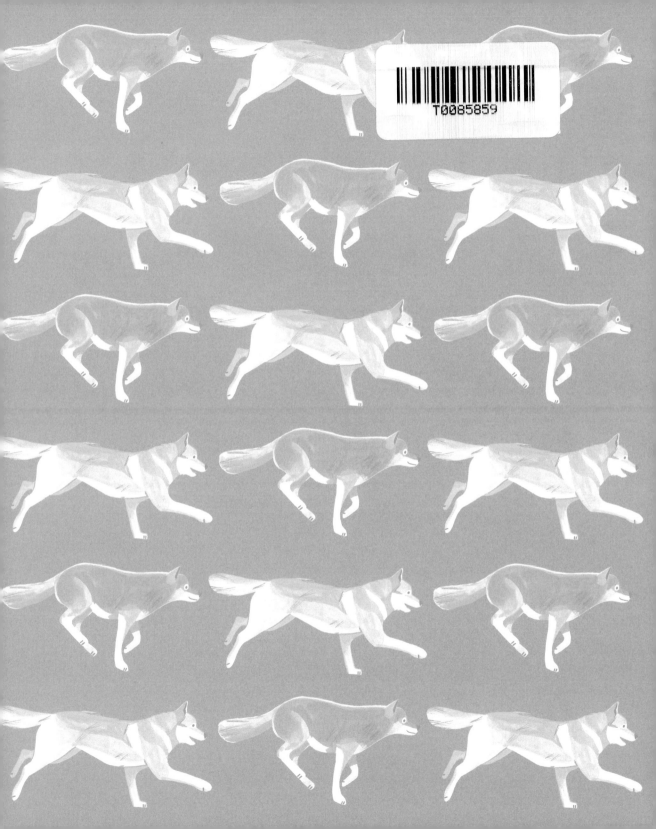

YOUNG ZOOLOGIST
GRAY WOLF

A FIRST FIELD GUIDE TO THE WILD DOG FROM THE WILDERNESS

NEON SQUID

CONTENTS

HELLO, YOUNG ZOOLOGIST!

Welcome to the wild world of gray wolves! People have been fascinated by wolves for thousands of years—we even domesticated their ancestors to create dogs. Although some people think wolves are scary, we have learned so much about them that says otherwise. They have a rich family life and play an important role in different ecosystems around the world. I first found out about these amazing creatures when I was very young, and now I study wolves in the wild. Even though we know a lot about wolves, there is still so much to discover! Let's head into the wilderness...

BRENNA CASSIDY

FACT FILE

SCIENTIFIC NAME
Canis lupus

CLASS
Mammal

LIFE SPAN
3–6 years

LOCATION
Northern areas of the world in Europe, Asia, and North America (the orange areas on this map).

HABITAT
Wolves live in a variety of different habitats, including the tundra, forests, mountains, and deserts.

TOP SPEED
35 mph (56 kph)

HEIGHT
26–32 in (66–81 cm) at the shoulder

WEIGHT
60–110 lb (27–50 kg). Males are usually 20% bigger than females.

EATS
Mostly large animals such as deer, elk, and moose, but they are not picky!

STATUS
Least Concern, but Endangered in some areas

BEFORE YOU GET STARTED

1

3

2

Sometimes pens won't work in extreme cold because the ink freezes! You can use pencils instead.

1 **BACKPACK**
You will need lots of gear and equipment in order to be comfortable outside and to do your research. A large, sturdy backpack is a great place to store everything.

2 **NOTEBOOK**
A notebook and a pen or pencil are important for writing down everything you observe. You will want to be able to remember your experiences so you can analyze them when you get back home.

3 **WARM CLOTHING**
It is often snowy and cold where wolves live. You need to bring warm clothes! Wolves can travel long distances, so good boots are a must if you want to follow them.

Wolves live in wild, remote places that can be tough to get to. You will need to bring some special gear to be safe while you study them—often in harsh conditions. Let's take a look at the equipment every wolf scientist can't go without.

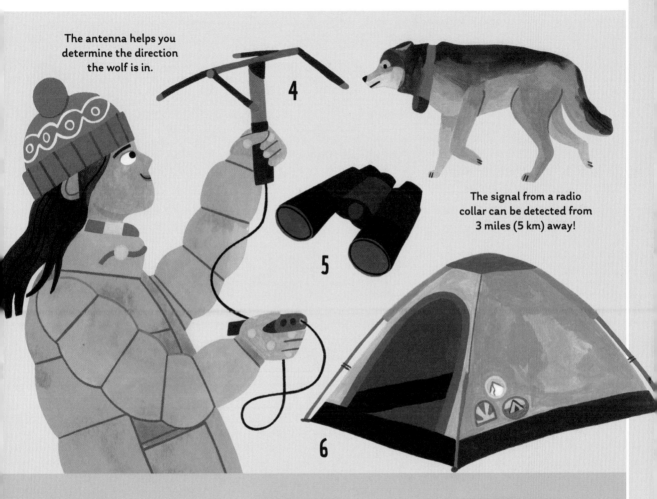

The antenna helps you determine the direction the wolf is in.

The signal from a radio collar can be detected from 3 miles (5 km) away!

4 ANTENNA
Some wolves have been fitted with radio collars so researchers can track their movements. An antenna is used to pick up the radio signals these collars give off.

5 BINOCULARS
Binoculars let you see long distances to spot wolves and their prey, which are the animals they eat. This will help you see wolves without disturbing them by being too close.

6 CAMPING GEAR
You may want to stay out for a few days, so a tent and sleeping bag will help you stay comfortable wherever you set up camp. You can even listen for wolves howling during the night!

MEET THE GRAY WOLF

STRONG JAWS

Wolves have strong jaws for hunting and eating. Their large front teeth, called canines, are made to grab and hold animals. Their back teeth, called molars, help crunch bones and chew meat.

THICK FUR

A wolf's thick, soft undercoat is perfect for keeping warm. Long outer fur on its back and neck protects it from snow and rain, keeping it dry.

WAGGING TAIL

Wolves use the position and movement of their tails to communicate their feelings. An excited wolf will wag its tail, while a scared wolf will tuck its tail between its legs.

Wolves have some amazing features that help them survive in the wild. From warm fur to an excellent nose, they are well suited to extreme environments. Here are a few of the reasons why these powerful hunters are so successful.

AMAZING EYESIGHT

Wolves can easily spot something moving very far away, which is helpful while hunting. They can't see the color red, but they have great night vision!

SENSE OF SMELL

Wolves can smell 100 times better than humans. Even so, they will still closely smell each other's rear end to get to know each other. To them it is like a very smelly handshake!

PADDED PAWS

A wolf's toes can spread apart and act like snowshoes to help them walk over snow and ice. Their claws are great for gripping steep hills.

DIFFERENT COLORS

Despite their name, gray wolves can be gray, black, or white, with brown or tan markings. Gray wolves are most common, while black wolves are only found in some areas. White wolves are only found in the Arctic.

9

LIFE IN THE PACK

OLDER SIBLINGS

The older siblings help the pack by learning to hunt and defend each other, but the most fun task they have is to play with the pups!

BREEDING FEMALE

Everyone listens to the mother of the pack, including the father. She makes most of the decisions about when and where the pack will travel, including where her den will be every year.

PUPS

Pups are constantly exploring and playing, which is great practice for being a grown-up. Adults will bring them fun things to play with, like antlers or bones. Even the adults will have fun playing with pups!

The largest known wolf pack had 37 members!

A wolf pack is a big, close family. This family is usually made up of a mother, father, their young, and other wolves that the pack adopts. They all work together to hunt, defend territory, and raise pups.

BREEDING MALE

The father of the pack is very good at hunting. While the mother of the pups is at the den, he and other members of the pack will hunt for food to bring back to her and the pups.

UNRELATED WOLVES

Wolf packs sometimes adopt unrelated wolves. They do everything other members do and are very dedicated to the pups and other members of their new pack. They are part of the family!

INJURIES

If a wolf is sick or injured, the rest of the pack can help them. They will protect the ill wolf from other animals and share their food with them until they are healed.

NEIGHBORHOOD WATCH

① HOWLING

Wolf packs will do everything they can to avoid a fight. Howling is a great way to announce their presence and let others know that they have a lot of members!

② CHASING AND FIGHTING

If howling does not scare off a rival pack, the trespassing wolves can be chased away. Whichever is the smaller pack is more likely to be chased away, and larger packs usually win any fights.

PATROLLING THE BORDERS

Wolf packs patrol the borders of their territory every one to two weeks to make sure other packs do not trespass. As they patrol they leave their scent behind by peeing on shrubs, trees, and rocks. They can also smell if any other packs have been through the area.

Wolves fiercely defend their pack's territory. They do this by howling at other packs, chasing them, or even fighting. These territories are passed down for generations, so defending them is a must!

3 VICTORY!

Older wolves in a pack have the knowledge and experience to know when to fight and when to flee—just like the adults in your life know how to protect you!

A pack can chase other wolves for more than 1 mile (2 km).

HOME SWEET DEN

PUPS IN THE DEN

Pups are born in an underground den that has been dug out by their mother. The den is usually one or more large chambers with a narrow entrance. This helps to keep out larger animals such as bears.

Dens can be used many times. A wolf mother may even use the den she was born in!

A den is a cozy, safe space where the pack lives until the pups are old enough to travel. While they're there, the adults hunt to feed the pups. As the pups grow older, they get braver and start to explore...

Adults can bring back up to 20 lb (9 kg) of food at a time.

ROAMING PUPS

When pups are a bit older, they will roam around the den area, exploring new sights and smells. They won't be alone though—there is always an adult babysitter (often an older sibling) nearby to protect and play with them.

PUPS ON THE PORCH

Pups spend two weeks in the den before venturing outside onto the porch. This is the area where dirt from inside was pushed out when the den was dug out. The pups will stick very close to the den, hiding inside if something scares them.

Dens are often near ponds or streams so the wolves have water to drink.

FINDING A NEW HOME

SETTING OUT

The decision to leave their pack is up to each wolf, and they sometimes try out smaller trips before leaving home for good. They may run into some scary things as they search for a new home, including people and other animals. Luckily they have learned a lot from their parents and siblings about how to stay safe. Will this wolf find somewhere new to call home?

Wolves usually avoid people and towns.

Wolves often leave home when they're between one and three years old.

SAFETY IN NUMBERS

Sometimes a group of brothers or sisters will leave their home in search of other wolves to form a new pack. Traveling in a group is much safer than going it alone.

Wolves need to stay away from animals that can be dangerous, such as bears.

Wolf parents teach their young how to hunt, raise pups, and protect their family. Then, when they're old enough, many young wolves will decide to leave their pack to find a mate and start families of their own.

These journeys can be up to 550 miles (885 km) long!

STAYING AT HOME

Male wolves leave the pack more often than female wolves. Females will stay at home because they might one day inherit their mother's leader position in the pack—and maybe even her den!

Wolves can travel over mountains, across rivers, and through deserts before finding a new home.

WILDLIFE BRIDGES

While traveling, a wolf needs to find a safe route. Humans can help by building bridges and tunnels made for wildlife over and under roads. This helps all the other animals crossing roads, too. Next time you are in a car, look out for places where animals can cross roads safely.

If a wolf is lucky, it will find another wolf and start a whole new pack.

LET'S CHAT

Living in a pack means wolves are constantly communicating with one another. They do this to show how they are feeling or to let others know they want to play! Wolves communicate with their body language, smells, and sounds.

A high, wagging tail means a wolf is happy and excited.

A still, low tail means a wolf is calm and relaxed.

Standing tall and showing teeth means a wolf is dominant and warns others to stay away.

Crouching and licking another wolf's face means a wolf is timid and submissive.

MOVE YOUR BODY

Wolves use the positions of their ears, tails, mouths, and bodies to communicate how they are feeling. Can you guess what these wolves are saying?

Wolves will bow to let others know they are ready to play!

SCENT MARKING

Wolves pee on lots of things to let other wolves know that they are in the area. They are more likely to leave scent marks on the edge of the pack's territory, rather than in the center. This creates a smelly fence around the territory!

Wolves often roll in smelly things, but we don't know why!

Scent marks can stay smelly for two to three weeks.

Pawing is a good way to get another wolf's attention.

HOWLING

Wolves howl to find each other, to tell other wolves to get away, and to bond with their pack. Wolf howls can be heard 6–9 miles (10–15 km) away! How loud can you howl?

ON THE HUNT

1 FINDING FOOD

Wolves hunt by traveling around looking for animals to eat. Unlike wild cats, they rarely try to sneak up on prey. Instead, they like to have prey run away from them—so they are less likely to be kicked by front hooves!

2 PICKING A TARGET

Wolves will chase a large group of prey to see if any individuals are slow, sick, or injured. A slower animal may be easier and less dangerous to hunt, so the wolves try to separate it from the others.

Wolves are carnivores, which means they mostly eat meat. To hunt large animals, wolves work together with amazing cooperation. Even the young wolves get involved—kind of like you helping prepare meals at your home!

3 THE CHASE

Smaller, faster female wolves are often at the front of the chase and will tire the prey out. The bigger, slower male wolves catch up later and help to bring the prey down. Working together helps wolf packs get more food.

ON THE MENU

Although wolves usually hunt large animals, they will eat most things. They have been seen eating berries, fish, and even beavers!

Hares and beavers are on the menu.

Sometimes wolves eat plants.

Coastal wolves catch fish.

Sometimes ravens playfully pull wolf tails.

RAVENS

Ravens and wolves have a special relationship. Ravens sometimes act like an alarm system for wolves, letting them know when there is danger nearby. They have also been seen playing with pups!

FRIENDS AND ENEMIES

Many other animal species live around wolves. Some of these animals try to stay far away from them, but others will follow wolves—hoping to get some leftover food. Let's see who is around!

Ravens can bond with one wolf pack and follow it around.

FOXES

Foxes will try to swipe food from wolves. Because foxes are so much smaller, they need to be careful not to be caught or they may get hurt!

COUGARS

Cougars try to stay out of the way of wolves for fear of being chased. If they do run into each other, the cougar will climb a tree and wait for the wolves to leave.

Ravens will hide wolf leftovers for when they are hungry later on.

GRIZZLY BEARS

Grizzly bears often steal food from wolf packs. Wolves will stick around while the bear eats, hoping to get a few bites. The wolves sometimes chase the bear and bite it on the rear!

BEETLES

Many types of beetle will happily feast on wolf meals. In total, 57 different beetle species have been found on the remains of animals wolves have eaten.

DOG ANCESTORS

Wolves may have initially approached humans in search of food.

THE ICE AGE

We don't know exactly how people domesticated (tamed) wolves in the first place. During the Ice Age a few brave wolves probably got closer and closer to human camps and eventually stayed. People may have also taken small wolf pups from their den and raised them as part of their family.

Dogs evolved from wolves about 20,000 years ago. That means if you have a pet dog it descended from wolves! As you know, wolf packs are families, so it didn't take long for wolves to accept people as their new packs.

DIFFERENT BREEDS

Although dog species now come in all shapes and sizes, they all started out looking like wolves! Despite their looks, dogs and wolves are still very closely related.

Chihuahua   Dachshund   Bulldog   Mastiff   Greyhound

WORKING DOGS

Dogs can help humans in many ways and even have some skills that wolves don't possess. Unlike wolves, dogs can understand people's facial expressions and what pointing at something means.

Service dogs help people with disabilities with different tasks.

Herding dogs help farmers move livestock from place to place.

Police dogs help solve crimes.

THE BIG BAD WOLF

FAIRY TALES

For centuries, people have used wolves to symbolize scary things. Wolves were often seen as a threat to the safety of people and as competition for food, and this fear led to the stories we hear today. Even though wolves are rarely aggressive to people, these beliefs have not gone away.

Wolves are in many fairy tales, myths, and stories—but they are usually mean or evil in them! Why might some people think wolves are bad? How many stories can you think of where wolves are the villain?

SCARY HUMANS

While wolves usually live in extremely wild places, humans have taken over a lot of their habitats. This means that these days wolves and people run into each other more often. Despite their fierce reputation, wolves avoid people as much as possible and are usually scared of them!

LEGENDARY WOLVES

Not everyone fears wolves. Many cultures around the world respect these amazing creatures as symbols of strength, loyalty, and courage. These cultures often have legends where wolves are the heroes of the story.

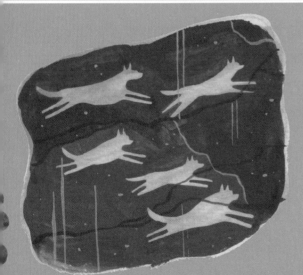

For many centuries, people have included wolves in their art. These ancient engravings come from Mongolia.

Legend says a mother wolf raised the founders of the city of Rome in Italy.

LOOKING TO THE FUTURE

RETURN TO YELLOWSTONE

Due to conflicts with people, wolves hadn't been seen in Yellowstone National Park, in decades. In 1995, 14 wolves were taken from Canada and released into Yellowstone. Since then, they have spread all over the Northern Rocky Mountains!

There are now about 100 wolves living in Yellowstone.

REWILDING

Returning animals to places where they used to live is called rewilding. Different animals evolved alongside wolves in Yellowstone. Without the wolves around, the ecosystem was out of balance. When the wolves were brought back, all sorts of interesting things started happening...

Wolves eat elk, and the elk became more cautious with the wolves around.

Willow trees grew taller because there were fewer elk around to eat them.

Beavers ate more willow trees. This meant they could dam more rivers, which improved river health!

Humans and wolves have not always gotten along. Today, however, people are working hard to bring wolves back to areas where they have not been seen for many years. They are finding new ways of living happily alongside wolves.

SAFE FARMING

Farmers can live alongside wolves by discouraging them from getting near their livestock. They do this not by hurting the wolves, but by using large dogs to protect livestock and flags to scare wolves away.

GET INVOLVED

You can help wolves too! Encourage people to learn about how wonderful wolves are—they're not at all like the scary creatures from fairy tales! You can also protect the places wolves live by helping to restore wild places. Maybe you could even see a wild wolf yourself one day!

Restoring places wolves live gives them room to raise pups and thrive.

Wild, protected places such as national parks are great places to see wolves.

GLOSSARY

Ancestor
A relative from a very long time ago.

Breeding
When species mate to produce offspring—in the case of wolves: pups!

Carnivore
An animal that eats meat. Dogs and cats are carnivores.

Den
A safe place where a mother wolf gives birth to her young, usually a hole dug in a hillside or under a tree or rock.

Domestication
The process of taming a species over many generations. Dogs and cats are domesticated.

Ecosystem
All of the living and nonliving things that make up an area.

Evolution
Gradual changes in the way species look or behave in order to better suit the environment they live in. These changes occur over a long period of time.

Herbivore
An animal that eats plants. Deer and horses are herbivores.

Ice Age
A time period long ago when Earth was very cold and many places were covered in large ice sheets.

Pack
A group of wolves that live, hunt, and travel together. They are often related to one another.

Predator
An animal that eats other animals to survive.

Prey
An animal that is eaten by other animals.

Pup
A young wolf that is less than one year old.

Rewilding
The process of turning an area back to a more natural and wild state. This includes bringing back animals that have not been there for a long time.

Scent marking
When wolves pee on a particular spot to let other wolves know they are in the area.

Territory
An area where wolves hunt and raise their young.

INDEX

This has been a

NEON 🦑 SQUID

production

Thank you to my family for fostering a little girl's curiosity about the natural world, and to the Yellowstone National Park Wolf Project for helping me turn that curiosity into a career. And to my own little wolf descendant at home, thank you for teaching me how a dog thinks, and loves.

Author: Brenna Cassidy
Illustrator: Sally Agar

Editorial Assistant: Malu Rocha
US Editor: Allison Singer Kushnir
Proofreader: Jane Simmonds

Copyright © 2023
St. Martin's Press
120 Broadway, New York,
NY 10271

Created for St. Martin's Press
by Neon Squid
The Stables, 4 Crinan Street,
London, N1 9XW

EU representative: Macmillan
Publishers Ireland Ltd,
1st Floor, The Liffey Trust Centre,
117–126 Sheriff Street Upper,
Dublin 1, D01 YC43

10 9 8 7 6 5 4 3 2 1

The right of Brenna Cassidy to
be identified as the author of
this work has been asserted in
accordance with the Copyright,
Designs and Patents
Act, 1988.

Library of Congress Cataloging-
in-Publication Data is available.

Printed and bound in
Guangdong, China by
Leo Paper Products Ltd.

ISBN: 978-1-684-49313-5

Published in September 2023.

www.neonsquidbooks.com